What Shape Is That?

by Anne O'Brien
illustrated by Suydam Studios

Orlando   Boston   Dallas   Chicago   San Diego

Visit *The Learning Site!*

www.harcourtschool.com

Every day, in everything we do,
there are shapes all around us. There
are circles, squares, rectangles, and
triangles. Look around you. Can you
find these shapes?

A circle is a completely round shape. A square is a shape with four straight sides. Each side of a square is the same length. A rectangle is also a shape with four straight sides. A rectangle has two long sides and two shorter sides. Squares and rectangles have four corners.

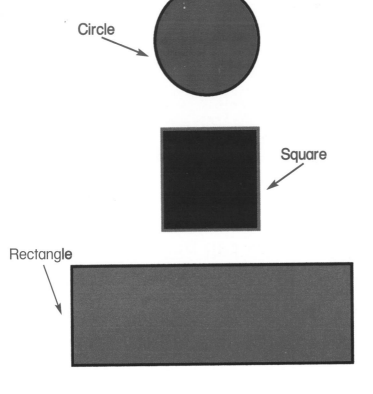

Circle

Square

Rectangle

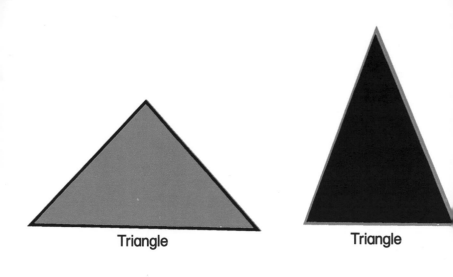

Triangle   Triangle

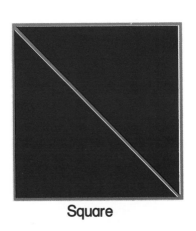

Square

A triangle is a shape with three sides. The sides can be the same length or different lengths. You can put two triangles with equal sides together to make a square.

4

Let's look at two picture frames.
One frame is shaped like a square.
One frame is shaped like a rectangle.
They both have four straight sides.
How can you tell which is the square
and which is the rectangle?

The frame shaped like a square has four sides that are all the same length. The frame shaped like a rectangle has two sides that are longer than the other two. So the picture frame with the cat is a square. The picture frame with the dog is a rectangle.

Now let's look for shapes around us. Let's start at home. Good morning! Your bed is a rectangle. Your window is a rectangle, too. Do you see the sun shining? It's a circle. The door to your room is a rectangle. The door knob is a circle.

Let's go to school. Your school
building might be a rectangle. A desk
is often a rectangle. Computer paper
often is shaped like a rectangle. A
chalk eraser is a rectangle. Almost all
the books are rectangles. School is full
of rectangles!

Of course, there are circles at school, too. The globe is a circle. The lids on the paint jars are circles. The little erasers on the ends of the pencils are shaped like circles.

Let's play sports at recess. A basketball is shaped like a circle. The hoop with the net is a circle, too. The basketball court is a rectangle. The seat of the bench you sit on is another rectangle.

Let's walk home after school. The wheels on the cars and bicycles are circles. The sidewalk is made up of squares. A house could be a square or a rectangle with a triangle roof on top.

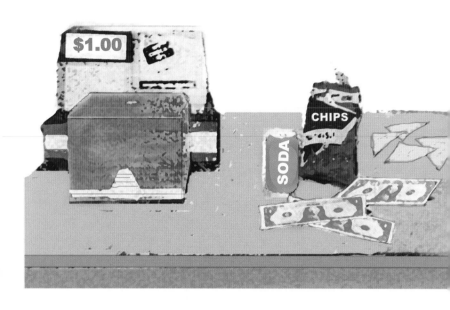

Let's stop at the store for a snack.
The top of a soda can is a circle.
Tortilla chips are shaped like triangles.
We use dollar bills and coins to pay
for the snacks. The dollars are
rectangles and the coins are circles.
There are shapes everywhere!

What shapes can we find when we listen to music at home? A tape cassette is a rectangle. What about a CD? A CD case is a square. What is inside the case? It's a round CD that is shaped like a perfect circle.

Let's order pizza for dinner. How many shapes can we find? The pizza comes in a box shaped like a square. The pizza inside the box is a circle. The circle fits inside the square, just like a round CD fits inside a square case.

14

If you cut the pizza into slices, the pieces look like triangles. How many triangles fit into this circle?

The napkins can be squares. If you fold a square in half, it makes a triangle. Then the two triangles together make a square.

It's time for bed. Do you see that circle outside your window? It's the full moon! You can read some rectangle pages in your rectangle book before you fall asleep. Goodnight! Your rectangle pillow is the last shape you'll see today!

16